THE DANGER

and

POWER

of

HIDDEN CURSES

Rev. James Solomon

ISBN 979-8-88832-752-4 (paperback)
ISBN 979-8-88832-753-1 (digital)

Christian Faith Publishing
832 Park Avenue
Meadville, PA 16335
www.christianfaithpublishing.com

Printed in the United States of America

This book is dedicated to the Holy Spirit,
the Helper of my soul
and the One behind all the revelations shared in this book.
To Him alone be glory, honor, and power
forever and ever. Amen.

He has come that you may have LIFE, *and that*
you may have it more ABUNDANTLY.

—John 10:10b

CONTENTS

ACKNOWLEDGEMENT

Discovering the importance of people in the pursuit of greatness is one of the best discoveries we can make in life. It is important to note that from the cradle to the grave, we will always need people who will help us to succeed and fulfill our divine destiny.

I want to express my appreciation to some people whom God has placed in my life to assist me in my journey toward greatness. This book is a joint effort of people who have believed in my vision and have contributed immensely in one area or the other to make it a reality.

I want to thank my father in the Lord, the late Rev. Dr. James Boyejo. Your life and ministry have greatly impacted my life for good, and I just can't forget you, sir. Pastor Enoch Adeboye, the general overseer of the Redeemed Christian Church of God (worldwide), is my mentor whose life and ministry have been a perfect example to me at all times. Sir, I love and appreciate the opportunity given to me to be a blessing to the body of Christ in the Redeemed Christian Church of God (worldwide). Thanks a lot for always being there for me.

I would like to express my appreciation to my faithful friends—Rev. Kayode Kolawole of Power House of Jesus Ministries, Ibadan (Nigeria); Evangelist Mike Okuo, AIG (retired), who is always a source of encouragement to me; and to my special friend Rev. Dr. Omomokuyo of Christ Anointed Kingdom Church, Lagos (Nigeria).

A big thanks to all my faithful pastors who are committed to the vision of Jesus People's Revival Ministries and Jesus Family Chapel in Nigeria, Kenya, Sierra Leone, and the United States of America.

CHAPTER 1

What Is a Curse?

A *curse* could be defined as

- an evil or a negative pronouncement;
- a violent expression of evil (intent) upon others;
- a word, phrase, or sentence calling for punishment, injury, or destruction of something or somebody;
- uttering an evil wish against someone;
- an evil pronouncement propelling one's life in a direction not originally intended;
- words put together to torment a person with great calamity;
- an invisible barrier that keeps people away from the plan of God for their lives; and
- oral pronouncements that bring about harm.

Curses could be

- self-inflicted,
- based on disobedience to the Word (and Spirit) of God,
- inherited,
- transferred, and
- pronounced on an individual by wicked people.

When hidden curses are in place, you find yourself taking wrong steps and making wrong decisions, and the spirit of failure will be in full operation.

I have discovered that many Christians have fasted, prayed, waited on God, and done many similar things that needed to be done, yet they are still looking or expecting a solution to their problems. One might be tempted to ask, "What is really going on? I have prayed all the prayers I know, I have gone through several deliverance sessions, I fasted, I've attended several revival meetings, and yet I am still waiting for a solution to my problem. Something is wrong somewhere." It is questions like this that prompted me to seek the Lord and ask Him why a large number of His children are still suffering, crying, and asking themselves what could be wrong with them. God's response to me is that a lot of His children are still under "hidden curses."

The curses are hidden because they cannot be seen—they are *concealed*. These hidden curses are obscure, unexplained, and undisclosed, meaning we are unaware of it, and it can neither be found nor be seen. For example, a good fighter—professional boxer or wrestler—goes into the ring for a match. Obviously, before the match, he must have trained hard and done everything necessary to prepare himself for the match or fight. Having done all, let's assume that on the day of the fight, the wrestler or boxer goes into the ring for the fight and cannot see his opponent. At the sound of the bell, he starts punching the air with all his might and dancing around the ring, displaying all his training skills. If he does this for about three hours nonstop, he will definitely collapse and pass out due to exhaustion without winning the match. Why? He had nobody to fight him or to contest with in the ring.

This example is actually the story of many Christians today; they don't see who they are fighting against or understand the battle they are fighting. As a result, they don't win. No matter how much strength, energy, practice, and training such people put into fighting these, they don't win. Rather, they collapse because if they cannot see the person (or situation) they are fighting against, they can't win.

This is why I am sharing this topic on "the power and danger of hidden curses."

If as a Christian you don't *see* a curse that is affecting you, does that curse have any power over you? Can a curse have power over you since you are unaware of its existence? You are unaware of a curse in your lineage and/or your life; can such a curse affect you? After all, if a man is unaware that a person could be killed by a motor vehicle (in an accident) and he gets into a vehicle, this will not stop him from getting killed by a motor vehicle.

CHAPTER 2

What Is a Hidden Curse?

Then answered all the people, and said, "His blood be on us, and on our children. (Matthew 27:25)

From this scripture, we can see that the children mentioned were not present at the time of this commitment. They were unaware of the dilemma and problems that their parents had heaped on them by this declaration or pronouncement. Will these children be affected later on in life by this pronouncement? YES! Will these children realize that they have a serious problem? Not until they find things working against them in life.

It is possible that some parents who made this pronouncement in **Matthew 27:25** did not have any children at the time of the pronouncement; while some might have children who were infants or toddlers. It is also possible that some of these people were not even married, yet they made such a pronouncement on themselves and their future children. Now, when they get married, settle down, and begin to have children, the curse will be waiting patiently to affect the lives of their children. These children will now grow up never knowing that their parents unconsciously evoked a curse upon them. It becomes a hidden curse to them because the curse was evoked or pronounced on them by their parents in the children's absence. The absence of the children at the time of pronouncement does not make the curse less effective or powerless in their lives. In case there is anyone reading this book who is going through a similar occurrence in his or her life today, there shall be deliverance for you in the name of Jesus.

Let us consider some scenarios. We find cases of some people, for example, residing in the United States of America who are in need of legal documentation to obtain a permanent residence status in the country (such as green card). Such people put together their paperwork with ease, and in no time, they receive their green card or citizenship. Meanwhile, you struggle to put your paperwork together, paying one lawyer after the other, and at the end, you end up with no positive result.

In a different scenario, we see ladies eligible for marriage finding their life partners with ease, and in no distant time, they get married, whereas you seem to be going in and out of one relationship after another with no prospects for marriage. In a similar scenario, we see couples who are happily married the first time around, but you are on your second or third marriage, and it is also turning out to be a disaster.

In all these scenarios, the main thing responsible for all these failures can be referred to as "hidden curses." These hidden curses are very powerful, whether you believe it or not, as curses carry the same power. One fact I will like to bring to your attention is that the length of time after a curse has been pronounced cannot affect the power of the curse. This means that even after the death of the person who was cursed, the curse still lives on; in other words, it outlives the intended victim. This is how serious and powerful a curse (hidden curse) is.

I remember the story of a very popular man in Lagos—one of the states in the western part of Nigeria—during one my crusades at the Onikan Stadium (also in Lagos). At the time, he was the general manager in charge of the stadium. He attended one of the programs and stayed all night till the wee hours of the morning when the program ended. Before leaving, he sent me a note saying he wanted to see me before I left the stadium to get my rest. I began to wonder what he wanted from me and thought that maybe being the manager of the stadium he wanted to increase my fee or tell me that I can't hold my program there the following week. So as early as 4:00 a.m. or 5:00 a.m., when the program ended, I rushed down to his office, where I found him still awake. Actually, when I got to his office, I found him sitting down, staring up at the ceiling. We exchanged greetings, and then he said that while listening to my teaching during the program, there was something I said that troubled him so much because it seemed to be the exact thing affecting his family. Then he went on to list the problems.

First, in his family, the male children do not succeed in anything. In spite of the level of education they attain (bachelor's degree, master's degree, etc.) or the honors they achieve, they will amount to nothing, and he is an example. He has two university degrees, but it took him a lot of struggle before he could get his present job as the stadium manager. Meanwhile, considering what he studied at the university, the position of general manager at the stadium is way beneath him, but he had to make do with it. He said he is the only male child in his family that made it up to that level; the other male members of his family are out on the street, wandering, drinking, and wasting away. In Lagos, this man will be referred to as "the son of the soil" because he hails from Lagos—born, bred, and raised in Lagos. He is actually from a very popular family that is well known in Lagos.

Second, at the age of eighteen, everyone born in this family experience terrible eye infirmity to the extent that some of them are unable to read. He showed me the pair of glasses he uses, and the lenses were very thick. He said after listening to me that night, he knew that what was happening in his family was the result of hidden curse. He believed that if I prayed with him, the curse will be lifted, and the family will be free.

So I told him that he should rally together all members of his family because I needed to meet with them. He said that wouldn't be a problem and he went ahead and arranged the meeting. We met at a venue in Surulere (a city in Lagos State)—all the members of his family, including the eldest family member who was about 102 years of age and completely blind. When we had sat down, I asked to speak with the old man first before we began to pray. Everyone present agreed. I then asked the old man to tell me things that he *knows* about the entire family that he would want us to pray about.

The old man paused for a while in deep thought and then answered, "My son, my own great-grandfather told me this story I'm about to tell you. He said that a long time ago on Carter Bridge (a well-known bridge in Lagos State named after President Jimmy Carter that leads into the island of Lagos), the beggars, lame, and blind men of the society used to line up on the bridge begging for alms. One day, while riding his horse across the bridge to Lagos Island, my great-grandfather became very angry and irritated at the sight of these beggars on the bridge. So he stopped and began shouting at them, saying that he has told them time and time again to go back to the city or village where they came from, but they refused to listen to him. Now he was going to teach them a lesson. He got down from his horse and began to chase them off the bridge. Those who could not run, he pushed them into the river beneath the bridge. The last of the beggars left on the bridge was a blind man who heard all that was said but didn't know where to run to. He began to cry out for help, but none came. My great-grandfather now approached the blind beggar where he was crying out for help and ordered him to be quiet, threatening to push him off the bridge like he had done the others. The blind beggar pleaded for mercy, telling my great-grandfather not to throw him into the river because he was blind. He continued and told the man that if he pushed him into the river, the man's children will not succeed or amount to anything in life, and that they will all go blind. As soon as he said this, my great-grandfather went ahead and pushed him into the river."

The old man narrating this story then said that from then onward, they all began to lose their sight at the age of eighteen.

The other children and members of the family who were present were amazed because they had never heard this story before. The Bible says,

> Thou shalt not curse the deaf, nor put a
> stumblingblock before the blind, but shalt fear
> thy God: I am the Lord. (Leviticus 19:14)

This blind beggar probably did not know this scripture, but he made a pronouncement on the man saying that his children will not succeed in life and they will be blind. These two specific pronouncements made by the blind beggar began affecting members of the family from that period up till this present generation. Until this revelation came forth, the children of this family, including the general manager who invited me, were unaware of the origin of their sufferings; who they knew was that none of them were making it in life. This pronouncement made years (and generations) ago upon this family is an example of a hidden curse.

There might have been some things that have affected your family years ago, maybe some pronouncement regarding the females in your mother's lineage. It could be a hidden curse placed on the males in your family. All these hidden curses can and will be broken by the power in the name of Jesus.

These hidden curses are usually concealed, so you know nothing about them; you don't even know that they exist. And since you are unaware of its existence, you can't pray about it. You can only talk and/or pray about what you know or are aware of. Having said this, the fact that you are unaware of the existence of a hidden curse doesn't mean it won't affect you.

I once met a young lady in Canada who approached me saying that I need to pray for her. She originally comes from the eastern part of Nigeria and from a particular tribe where it is the belief that there is a curse on her family. She said everything she set out to do or lay her hands on has always failed to the point that she began to wonder if this is a result of the curse on her family that she has heard about. It was also said that they were not allowed to marry from families of other eastern tribes because of the curse on their family. I agreed with her in prayers, and the Lord destroyed the bondage of curses in her life. The origin of hidden curses is unknown to us, but God is able to deliver.

Today, the power of hidden curses affecting
my life shall be broken in the name of Jesus.

CHAPTER 3

What Is a Generational Curse?

A generational curse

- is a curse activated into one's life right from his/her birth, bringing that person into the same calamity affecting the family from generations past;
- is a curse you don't obtain through hard work; it automatically takes over a person's life;
- is a curse that is transferred from one parent to another within the same bloodline;
- is a curse that justifies the visitation of the sins of the ancestors on their children; and
- is a curse that operates from the bloodline of a person.

Looking back, each of us has two parents, four grandparents, eight great-grandparents, and sixteen great-great-grandparents—that is a total of thirty ancestors from which curses could possibly be derived or generated from.

> Thou shalt not make unto thee any graven image, or any likeness of anything that is in heaven above, or that is in the earth beneath, or that is in the water under the earth.

Thou shalt not bow down thyself to them, nor serve them: for I the LORD thy God am a jealous God, visiting the iniquity of the fathers upon the children unto the third and fourth generation of them that hate me;

And shewing mercy unto thousands of them that love me, and keep my commandment. (Exodus 20:4–6)

Examples of the Effect of Generational Curses

- Children talking and behaving like their parents
- Family-inherited diseases
- Children experiencing similar tragedies, mishaps, or situations as their parents
- Finding the source of inexplicable diseases within the family lineage
- Adam and Eve being cursed, but the curse rubbed off on all generations after them
- Canaan being cursed by Noah, but the descendants of Ham suffered the same calamity
- Reuben being cursed by his father, Jacob, but it was his descendants that suffered for it

Examples of Curses in the Bible

Below is a list of curses that need to be broken off your life and generation. To break these curses, according to **Galatians 3:13**, ask the Lord to forgive you (and your ancestors going back ten generations on both sides of your bloodline) for the sins and iniquities that allowed these curses to come upon you in JESUS'S NAME.

- Those who curse or mistreat Jews (**Deuteronomy 27:26; Genesis 12:3, 27:29; Numbers 24:9**)
- Those willing deceivers (**Joshua 9:23; Jeremiah 48:10; Malachi 1:14; Genesis 27:12**)

- An adulterous woman (**Numbers 5:27**)
- Disobedience of the Lord's commandments (**Deuteronomy 11:28; Daniel 9:11; Jeremiah 11:3**)
- Idolatry (**Jeremiah 44:8; Deuteronomy 5:8–9, 29:19; Exodus 20:5**)
- Those who keep or own cursed objects (**Deuteronomy 7:25; Joshua 6:18**)
- Those who refuse to come to the Lord's help (**Judges 5:23**)
- House of the wicked (**Proverbs 3:33**)
- He who gives nothing to the poor (**Proverbs 28:27**)
- The earth by reason of man's disobedience (**Isaiah 24:3–6**)
- Jerusalem is a curse to all nations if the Jews rebel against God (**Jeremiah 26:6**)
- Thieves and those who swear falsely by the Lord's name (**Zechariah 5:4**)
- Ministers who fail to give the glory to God (**Malachi 2:2; Revelation 1:6**)
- Those who hearken unto their wives rather than God (**Genesis 3:17**)
- Those who lightly esteemed their parents (**Deuteronomy 27:16**)
- Those who make graven images (**Deuteronomy 5:8, 27:15; Exodus 20:4**)
- Those who willfully cheat people out of their property (**Deuteronomy 27:17**)
- Those who take advantage of the blind (**Deuteronomy 27:18**)
- Those oppressing strangers, widows, and the fatherless (**Deuteronomy 27:19; Exodus 22:22–24**)
- He who lies with his father's wife (**Deuteronomy 27:21; Exodus 22:19**)
- He who lies with his sister (**Deuteronomy 27:22**)
- Those who smite their neighbors secretly (**Deuteronomy 27:24**)
- Those who take money to slay the innocent (**Deuteronomy 27:24**)

- He who lies with a beast (**Deuteronomy 27:21; Exodus 22:19**)
- Adulterers (**Job 24:15–18; Deuteronomy 22:22–27**)
- The proud (**Psalm 119:21**)
- Those who trust in man and not the Lord (**Jeremiah 48:10**)
- He who keeps back his sword from blood (**Jeremiah 48:10; 1 Kings 20:35–42**)
- Those who reward evil for good (**Proverbs 17:13**)
- Illegitimate children (**Deuteronomy 23:2**)
- Children born from incestuous unions (**Genesis 19:36–38**)
- Murderers (**Exodus 21:14**)
- Those who murder indirectly (**Exodus 21:14**)
- Children who strike their parents (**Exodus 21:15**)
- Kidnappers (**Exodus 21:16; Deuteronomy 24:7**)
- Those who curse their parents (**Exodus 21:17**)
- Those who cause the unborn to die (**Exodus 21:22–23**)
- Those who do not prevent death (**Exodus 2:29**)
- Those involved in witchcraft (**Exodus 22:18**)
- Those who sacrifice to false gods (**Exodus 22:20**)
- Those who turn people away from the Lord (**Deuteronomy 13:6–9**)
- Those who follow HOROSCOPES (**Deuteronomy 17:2–5**)
- Those who rebel against pastors (**Deuteronomy 17:12**)
- False prophets (**Deuteronomy 18:19–22**)
- Women who were not virgins before marriage (**Deuteronomy 22:13–21**)
- Parents who do not discipline their children but honor them above God (**1 Samuel 2:17, 27–36**).
- Those who curse their rulers (**1 Kings 2:8–9; Exodus 22:28**)
- Those who teach rebellion against the Lord (**Jeremiah 28:16–17**)
- Those who refuse to warn others against sin (**Ezekiel 3:18–21**)

- Those who defile the Sabbath **(Exodus 31:14; Numbers 15:32–36)**
- Those who sacrifice human beings **(Leviticus 20:2)**
- Participants in séance and fortune-telling **(Leviticus 20:6)**
- Homosexual and lesbian relationships **(Leviticus 20:13)**
- Sexual intercourse during menstruation **(Leviticus 20:18)**
- Necromancers and fortune tellers **(Leviticus 20:27)**
- Those who blaspheme the Lord's name **(Leviticus 24:15–16)**
- Those who are carnally minded **(Romans 8:6)**
- Sodomy (oral and anal sex) **(Genesis 19:13, 24–25)**
- Rebellious children **(Deuteronomy 21:18–21)**
- Possibly from murder or nonproductivity, a fugitive vagabond **(Genesis 4:11; Matthew 5:21–22)**
- Possible curse upon improper family structure—destruction of family priesthood—with special attention given to the relationship between father and children **(Malachi 4:6)**
- An undeserved (causeless) curse shall not come **(Proverb 26:2).**
- Any sin worthy of death is also cursed by the Lord **(Deuteronomy 21:22–23).**

Blotting out the handwriting of ordinances that was against us, which was contrary to us, and took it out of the way, nailing it to the cross; And having spoiled principalities and powers, he made a shew of them openly, triumphing over them in it. (Colossians 2:14–15)

Now the LORD had said unto Abram, Get thee out of thy country, and from thy kindred and from thy father's house, unto a land that I will shew thee: And I will make of thee a great nation, and I will bless thee, and make thy name great; and thou shalt be a blessing: And I will bless them that bless thee, and curse him that

curseth thee: and in thee shall all families of the
earth be blessed. (Genesis 12:1–3)

Descendants of Ada Take

A woman was born in 1740 named Ada Take. She died a con-
firmed drunkard and altogether had 700 descendants. Among the
descendants were 100 children born out of wedlock, 181 women
of the street, 142 beggars, 46 workhouse inmates, and 76 criminals.
This woman cost the country an estimated $1,200,000.

The Jukes family

There has been a careful research into the history of one of the
criminal families known as the Jukes. This family has a long and
conspicuous record of profligacy, insanity, prostitution, and drunk-
enness. A total of 1,200 descendants have been traced back to this
family: about 400 of these descendants were physically self-wrecked,
310 of them were professional paupers, 130 were convicted criminals, 60 were habitual thieves and pickpockets, and 7 of them were
murderers. Of the 1,200 descendants, only 20 of them learnt a trade,
and half of them owed it to prison discipline.

Andrew Murray's home

In the family of Andrew Murray of South Africa, 11 children
grew up into full adult life. Five of his sons became ministers of the
gospel, while 4 of his daughters became wives to ministers of the
gospel. The next generation had a more striking record: 10 grandsons
became ministers, and 13 grandchildren became missionaries. The
secret of this unusual contribution to the Christian ministry was the
Christian home of Andrew Murray.

Descendants of Jonathan Edwards

Jonathan Edwards was the son of a godly home. His father was a preacher, and so was his mother's father. Looking at the history of the offspring of this godly man, out of the 400 descendants that had been traced, 14 of them were college presidents; 100 of them were professors; 100 of them were either ministers of the gospel, missionaries, and/or theological teachers; about 100 of them were lawyers and judges; 60 of them were doctors; and many more were high-ranking authors or editors of journals. In fact, almost every conspicuous American industry has had one or more of Edwards' offspring as its promoters since the remote ancestor was married in the closing half of the seventeenth century.

CHAPTER 4

The Danger of Hidden Curses

The dangerous aspect of hidden curses is that one is not aware of it, and the fact that you are unaware of it doesn't make it ineffective. It is so important for us today to decree and/or demand that every hidden curse working against our lives should be broken permanently in the name of Jesus. In the book of Joshua, we read the following:

> And Joshua adjured them at that time, saying, "Cursed be the man before the Lord, that riseth up and buildeth this city Jericho: he shall lay the foundation thereof in his firstborn, and in his youngest son shall he set up the gate of it." (Joshua 6:26)

This was a pronouncement (curse) made by Joshua; there was no incantation or ceremony involved in this pronouncement—it was just a word released casually by Joshua. As harmless or casual as it seems, one would have thought that it won't be effective. Ten (twenty, a hundred, four hundred) years later, nobody rebuilt the walls or the city, yet the curse was effective. The length of time involved doesn't deactivate the power of a curse.

Another danger of curses is that it reverses God's divine order for your life; it can change or destabilize God's plans for your life and/or destiny. In the book of Genesis, Adam and Eve were told to succeed—who blessed them? It was the same God Who created them that told them to be fruitful and multiply, to have dominion, and so on. This was the original plan of God for their lives, which was supposed to last forever. When they disobeyed God, curses set in and caused a demarcation between them and God's blessings and original plans for their lives. Their story changed and their lives became the curse that was pronounced on them—that is, they will toil and labor before they eat, have untold pain and suffering during childbirth, and so on. I once shared a joke saying that God has delivered us from the curse of the law, and so when women want to give birth, it will be smooth, quick, easy, and pain-free. A sister heard this joke and actually believed what I said. She got married and, soon after, got pregnant. On the day of her delivery, she was in so much pain that she almost cursed me when she remembered the joke I had shared. She kept saying, "This is not what Pastor said. He said that it will be easy. Please, someone call Pastor for me." The curses were pronounced, and it cut off the blessings and changed the course of the lives of Adam and Eve up till our present generation. Curses are very dangerous, delicate, and powerful.

Going back to our case study in the book of Joshua—the curse had been pronounced, and the man who made the pronouncement had died. All the people (a whole generation) who heard the curse when it was made were all dead. A man called Hiel (from a later generation) rose up and decided to rebuild the gate of the city (of Jericho). He felt that if no one cared, he would do something about it. He decided to invest his time and money into a bit of community service—after all, the gate in question was for the city, not his own personal house. So his actions were legally and morally upright but saddled with a curse.

This brings me to the subject of the "will of God." Everything may look good, the intentions may be noble, but first of all, you need to find out if it is the will of God. No matter how decent the action might be, if it is not the will of God, then you have no business getting involved in it. This man, Hiel, did not pray or seek out God's will. He saw a problem or a need and had the money to invest in the project, so he went ahead and started building. Let me pause here a bit and ask this question: was Hiel aware that there was a curse pronounced on anyone who rebuilds the gate or the city? The answer is NO! He was unaware. You might ask how I know that he was unaware. First, he was not born at the time the curse was pronounced. Second, the curse was pronounced about five hundred years before his time. Third, those who would have told him about the curse were dead. Fourth, this curse was a hidden curse; he just saw an opportunity for investment. If a thing looks good outside the will of God, let it go— do not get involved. This is what affected Hiel. He was a cheerful man, given to God's work and building communities.

> In his days (of King Ahab) did Hiel the Bethelite build Jericho: he laid the foundation thereof in Abiram his firstborn, and set up the gates thereof in his youngest son Segub, according to the word of the Lord, which he spake by Joshua the son of Nun. (1 Kings 16:34)

If Hiel had a hint of the curse attached to the rebuilding of the city of Jericho, I don't think he would have embarked on that project. If he knew that rebuilding the city would cost him his firstborn and his lastborn, he would never have gone ahead with it. Among our children, the firstborn and lastborn are the ones usually considered most precious. This proves that he was unaware of the curse.

> The Lord God Almighty will keep our firstborns, lastborns, and or children safe. He will make them great. They will not die young and you will eat the fruit of your labor, in Jesus's name.

A lot of us find ourselves under hidden curses without knowing where they come from or that they exist, yet we are suffering for it. That we don't know about it or that it exists doesn't matter. Some women have suffered a series of miscarriages, and they don't know why. I clearly can relate to some of the situations a lot of you might be going through. My mother was married to another man, and then my father snatched her from her husband and married her. She got pregnant for my father, but that baby did not survive. She then got pregnant a second time, and I was born (you can read up on the rest of this story in my book *Deliverance from Demonic Covenants and Curses*).

We might be unaware of the origin of some of the problems we face in life, but we need to know that somewhere along the line, there might be a curse involved which is hidden to you (it may even be hidden from your parents). Whether you or your parents are aware of the existence of a curse, it is still powerful, effective, and dangerous, but you can be delivered from it.

> Heavenly Father, by the power in the power in the blood of Jesus, I deactivate the power of hidden curses affecting me, in the name of the Father, the Son, and of the Holy Ghost, in Jesus' name.

The story in the case study that we have just considered is about a curse that originated in the community. It wasn't Hiel's father that released a curse in his life; it was the community he belonged to that was cursed. Unknown to him, there was a curse on the project he embarked on. Unconsciously, some of us are handling projects that are cursed. The *buildings* you are trying to erect or the good deed you were trying to do have a laid-down curse attached to it. Some things we touch have curses attached to them, which are unknown to us, and the fact that we are unaware of these curses doesn't mean we won't suffer—ignorance is no excuse. That you don't know that a car is cursed doesn't guarantee that it will not knock you down. The good news is that today, you can be delivered by the power in the blood of Jesus.

Hiel got his own problems from the community he belonged to. In other words, if the nation or city you hail from has a curse on it, you will most likely face certain hidden curses in your life. Even though you are unaware of the curse placed on your town or country because it is hidden, the fact that you originated from that locality will make you struggle and suffer in life. Even if your own father or mother was not cursed particularly, you might still find the curses effective in your life because you are a part of the community.

> Heavenly Father, I release the blood of Jesus to my community, my city, or the family I originated from. Let all hidden curses, concealed curses, undisclosed curses that are affecting me be broken NOW in the name of Jesus.

This is why Christians should pray for the will of God. Assuming Hiel went to God in prayers, saying, "Father, I have the money to embark on this project (rebuilding the city), but I need to know your will. I don't want to invest my money into something that will ruin my career. Lord, show me your will. I am so interested in rebuilding this city, but I need to know if this is your will," do you think his firstborn son would have died had he taken his desire to God in prayer? Christians, please seek the will of God.

CHAPTER 5

The Power of Hidden Curses

Let's look at another case study. The Lord clearly ministered this point to my heart, and I want you to pray this prayer:

> Lord, reveal every hidden curse unknown to
> my parents or to my family, and all hidden curses
> that have brought my life to a standstill, reveal
> them to me and break it.

Around 90 percent of the battles that Christians face in life today are a result of a hidden curse. You can throw punches and win the battle only when you can see the person you are fighting with. The Apostle Paul said,

> I therefore so run, not as uncertainly; so fight
> I, not as one that beateth the air. (1 Corinthians
> 9:26)

This is the reason why marriages do not work out and end up in divorce, or some marriages work out but there are no children to show for it. I met someone who had lived in London for seven years and has been living in Canada for thirteen years; this person has no papers or legal document of her stay in the country (the equivalent of the US green card or citizenship). Every time she is on the verge of getting her papers, a new law will be passed which disqualifies her from getting her papers. I had a counseling session with this woman, and she revealed to me that even while she was back home in Nigeria attending primary school, things did not seem to work out for her. When the time comes for her to write an examination, she will suddenly fall ill, and this blocked her chances for success and promotion. During my last ministerial visit to Canada, the lady happened to be at the program where I was ministering. During the program, I ministered to her, and the power of God fell upon her mightily. I told her what the Lord revealed to me concerning her, and after that day, the light of God shone upon her life. She called me a week later saying that she had been waiting for her immigration papers for the past thirteen years, and miraculously, the letter she had been expecting arrived in the mail after one weekend of prayers. Beloved, the things you might have been struggling for over forty-one years, when the power of hidden curses are broken, you will have your testimony.

> And Abraham journeyed from thence toward the south country, and dwelled between Kadesh and Shur, and sojourned in Gerar. And Abraham said of Sarah his wife, She is my sister: and Abimelech King Gerar sent, and took Sarah. (Genesis 20:1–2)

We can see that even from the Bible days, men have always been in trouble when they get married to beautiful women. They don't realize that marrying a beautiful woman results in *beautiful problems.* So we see in this scripture we just read that Abraham had problems because of the beautiful woman he was married to. Before they arrived at the city, he confided in her and told her that in order to save his life, she should say she is his sister and not his wife when asked who she was; also, he was afraid that someone would take her away from him. Men, you need to relax and know that it is God that keeps the woman, and that there is really not much you can do to keep a woman from leaving. If a woman is not kept by God and she chooses to live out her old sinful nature committing all sorts of atrocities, there's not much a man can do but give her his full support. The man should simply commit the woman unto God.

So Abraham had this similar problem. When they got to the city, the king, who was obviously captivated by Sarah's beauty, requested that Sarah be brought to him. He was unusually busy with his kingly duties that day, so he asked that she be kept in his guest room.

> But God came to Abimelech in a dream by
> night, and said to him, "Behold, thou art but a
> dead man, for the woman which thou hast taken;
> for she is a man's wife." (Genesis 20:3)

King Abimelech must have replied or even argued with God, telling Him that He was mistaken because the woman (Sarah) that he had with him was not married; Sarah herself said she was not married, and even Abraham said she is not his wife.

> But Abimelech had not come near her: and
> he said, "Lord, wilt thou slay also a righteous
> nation? Said he not unto me, She is my sister?
> And she, even she herself said, He is my brother:
> in the integrity of my heart and innocency of my
> hands have I done this." And God said unto him
> in a dream, "Yea, I know that thou didst this in
> the integrity of thy heart; for I also withheld thee
> from sinning against me: therefore suffered I thee
> not to touch her. Now therefore restore the man
> his wife; for he is a prophet, and he shall pray for
> thee, and thou shalt live: and if thou restore her
> not, know thou that thou shalt surely die, thou,
> and all that are thine." (Genesis 20:4–7)

Christian women, the strongest weapon you possess is prayer. If your husband decides to go after another woman, telling her he is divorced or on the verge of divorce and so on, let him be. If you truly trust in the Lord God Almighty that we serve, then know that God will fight for you. From the passage above, both Abraham and Sarah lied, and King Abimelech was justified, but God stepped in for Abraham. He didn't even have to fight; this battle was now between God and Abimelech. If you know the right weapon to use, God will fight for you. No matter the games, lies, or tricks that a man or woman may put up, as long as you have God on your side, He will fight for you.

And so God told Abimelech to restore Sarah back to Abraham. In addition, he was to ask Abraham to pray for him so that his life and the lives of his entire household will be spared. Even though Abraham lied, God insisted that Abimelech ask Abraham to pray for him. One interesting thing about God is that once He is interested in you, if anyone speaks evil against you (whether justified or not), such a person is in trouble with God. When God is especially interested in your case even in the midst of your mistakes, whoever curses you will be in danger.

It's amazing to know how many curses have been inflicted on certain individuals because the head (father, grandfather, great-grandfather, etc.) of the family took the wife of another man. These now becomes hidden curses. When Abimelech took Sarah, he asked God if He would indeed kill (slay) a righteous nation when he hadn't even slept with Sarah. And God answered yes, even though He prevented Abimelech from sleeping with Sarah. One can see God fighting for Abraham in this case, so why would you waste your time fighting your battles? If you trust God enough, He will fight for you. After Abimelech took Sarah, who began to talk to him? Was it Abraham? Did Abraham quarrel with him or take him to court? No! It was God by Himself that did all the talking and the fighting for Abraham.

Men, raise your right hand and say this prayer:

> Father, concerning my marriage, fight for me. I refuse to fight this battle anymore. Lord, fight for me in Jesus's name.

Women, raise your right hand and say this prayer:

> In the name of the Father and of the Son and of the Holy Ghost, concerning my marriage,

I will not fight anymore. You will fight for me in
Jesus's name.

Abraham and Sarah lied to Abimelech, who in his own right
was an honest man—he saw what he liked and made inquiries before
claiming the object of his attention. Yet God said Abraham was to
pray for Abimelech. Sometimes, it is hard to understand the order
of God. Being close to ministers of the gospel, one tends to see their
humanity and weaknesses. People tend to think that it is the pastor
or minister that blesses people with miracles and answers prayers.
No! The minister or pastor is just a vessel that God uses. God does
not look at them the way we do. Remember what God says,

> "For my thoughts are not your thoughts,
> neither are your ways my ways," saith the Lord.
> (Isaiah 55:8)

God does not see the weaknesses in the ministers of the gospel;
He sees His spirit in them. And this is why He told Abimelech to
ask Abraham to pray for him (in spite of his weakness); otherwise,
Abimelech would have been cursed by God.

> So Abraham prayed unto God: and God
> healed Abimelech, and his wife, and his maid-
> servants; and they bare children. For the Lord
> had fast closed up all the wombs of the house
> of Abimelech, because of Sarah Abraham's wife.
> (Genesis 20:17–18)

And so we see that Abraham prayed for God, and God answered
and healed Abimelech. In spite of his weaknesses, Abraham prayed,
and healing came forth. Not only was Abimelech healed, but his wife
was also healed. You might ask why his wife was in need of healing; what sin did she commit? This goes to show that we are often
unaware of the things that happened in our lives, which opened the
door to curses. In marriages today, it is possible that either the man

or the woman has brought some hidden curses into the family from their activities outside the home, and the annoying part of it is that the spouse is usually unaware of these activities or the hidden curses they produce. Just like we see in the case of Abimelech—the king committed the sin, yet his wife's womb became barren. In fact, the wombs of all the women within Abimelech's palace became barren. If, for instance, there was a female chef who comes in to work every day at the palace, she will eventually go home barren just by virtue of working in the king's palace. All the workers on the king's payroll will also partake of this curse of barrenness. Maybe some young newly wedded couple was invited by the king to spend their honeymoon at his palace. By the time they leave to go home and start their married life, the woman is barren, and they won't know how or where the problem came from.

You might have visited certain places; spent the night in certain houses, homes, or hotels; or worked at certain companies or offices that harbor hidden curses that were unknown to you—all of which have affected your life. By the power in the name of Jesus, those curses shall be broken! Another example is a scenario where you buy chicken from a place that has been cursed with barreness (like Abimelech's palace) with the intention of setting up a poultry business. You need to understand that even the female animals were partakers of the curse. Now you have invested so much money into the business with no profit and nothing to show for it until you find yourself financially at level zero. This takes me back to what we have discussed earlier on in this book—knowing the will of God on any matter; this is very important.

Look back and examine your own family and ask yourself how many chiefs, elders, or family heads have done something in the past which brought about hidden curses within the family. Due to the fact that they are the ones in positions of authority over the family, they have brought in curses within the entire family because of what they have done. There is deliverance for you in Jesus's name.

There is a small city in Nigeria (West Africa), which was always being attacked and conquered by this particular big city that would raid them and plunder all their goods. The inhabitants of this small city would cry and lament because they were powerless against this big city. One day, an inhabitant of this small city decided that he had had enough of the onslaught from the big city. He went into personal training and trained some of the young men in the city so that they avenge their city. When he and his crew were ready, they went to the big city and fought and defeated them. This made the man very happy because he concluded that the people of the big city will no longer attack them. On his way back home to the small city, he and his entourage were rejoicing, singing, and dancing. As they approached the gate to the small city, the man was expecting to see all the inhabitants waiting to rejoice and celebrate with him; after all, he won the victory for the small city. Alas, when they got to the gate, nobody from the small city showed up. He became so furious that he stood at the gate and declared that from that day, because no one came out to appreciate what he had done for the city, no child born in that city will bring success to that city. They might become successful anywhere on this earth, but they will not bring their success into that city. After making this declaration, he died at the entrance to the city. It is on record that up till this very day, people from this small city are successful entrepreneurs in different countries all over the world, but that city is nothing to write home about. Even when some of the indigenes come home to set up some business or to do something to improve the outlook of the city, all their efforts fail woefully, and nothing gets done or achieved—all because of a pronouncement made by that man.

Father, by the power in the blood of Jesus,
I deactivate every hidden curse that is currently
affecting my life, in the name of Jesus.

CHAPTER 6

Inherited Family Curses

A lot of people stumble through life without being able to fully tap into the various blessings that God has prepared for them. They stagger from one serious problem to another, from one major disaster to another, and they never achieve their full potentials. If such people were to be factories or manufacturing companies, their capacity utilization would never go above 20 or 30 percent at any point in their lifetime. In almost all these cases, the cause of bondage is usually not their fault; the source of their problems can be traced to curses inherited and passed down the family line from their ancestors or forefathers. Even more painful is the fact that most people or families struggling under such curses are blissfully ignorant of the source of their troubles.

You can easily see a clear pattern in families that suffer from inherited curses; certain peculiar problems occur from generation to generation. For instance, poverty could be endemic in the family. From generation to generation, the family turns out lines of paupers, people who are so poor they barely survive from one day to the next. In some other cases, it could be that the members of the family always get married very late in life, or that members of the family tend to die at a young age—they don't live beyond forty-five years of age.

If your family falls within a particular category, upon deep scrutiny of your life and progress, you may be shocked to find that you are heading for a similar end. For example, if you are mature in age yet are still unmarried, you are well on your way to confirming the recurring pattern of late marriages within the family. In that case, it is likely that you have inherited a family curse.

I came across a woman who discovered a particular truth about her family before it was too late for her. She came to me for counseling and prayers; according to her story, every first male child born into her family died around the age of forty. If the firstborn was a female, at about that same age, she would go insane. Without a doubt, this was an inherited family curse, and I told her so. The truth helped her. We knew how and where to direct our prayers of deliverance. God rolled the curse away from her life. She is now over fifty years old and she is alive, healthy, and well.

There are different examples of how inherited family curses wreak havoc in the lives of many unsuspecting Christians. Sometimes, it takes a thorough examination of one's life, situation, and family to know that there is a problem. Occurrences that you think are not important may turn out to be very pivotal to your progress. For example, if your father found it difficult to live with one wife, even if you are married to a queen, the same fate is likely to befall you unless you break it. If you are a woman and your mother was the type that went from one man to another and was never really able to settle down, even if your husband gives you the whole world, the evil spirits operating in your family lineage will drive you out of wedlock, unless the power of the Lord breaks their grip.

In some families, nobody becomes successful in life despite all the money invested to obtain the best form of education available. In other families, every old person loses their sight at a certain age, and if you are at that age in your family, you need to examine yourself. You are certain to have that same problem even if you are a born-again Christian!

If an inherited curse is at work, you are bound to suffer its consequences, except you pray the prayer of deliverance to break this curse. Unfortunately, many people who suffer these predicaments pray incorrectly because they are ignorant of the sort of battle with which they are confronted.

CHAPTER 7

The Root Cause of Inherited Family Curses

Idol Worship

The main cause of family curses is the sin of idol worship. Concerning this, God explicitly warns:

> Thou shalt have no other gods before Me.
> Thou shalt not make unto thee any graven image, or any likeness of anything that is in heaven above, or that is in the earth beneath, or that is in the water under the earth.
> Thou shalt not bow down thyself to them, nor serve them: for I the LORD thy GOD am a jealous God, visiting the iniquity of the fathers upon the children unto the third and fourth generation of them that hate me. (Exodus 20:3–5)

The warning is clear, unequivocal, and unambiguous. God said we should neither worship nor serve idols. He says if we do, He will visit the iniquities on succeeding generations. It is immaterial whether you are ignorant of the consequences of your actions or not; that is not God's problem. When God says something, He means it and He does it; He keeps to His Word.

Note, therefore, that every time you secretly visit the fetish priest, star readers, and astrologers or participate in some false religion, you are bringing curses on the lives of your children. And these curses will pass from generation to generation for four hundred years. The curses could attract poverty, sickness, diseases, or marital problems. Whatever the case, these curses will last for four generations.

My own life aptly illustrates this fact. My father was an idol worshipper, and my life was miserable until 1987 when God delivered me. The vicious cycle of trials and tribulations that I underwent is the usual fate that awaits the children of witch doctors, Alfas (Muslim clerics), traditional warriors and rulers, cult members, and those who worship idols in whatever form, including the practice of Halloween. Offspring who achieve some measure of success in life will be brought down at one point or the other because God is a jealous God "visiting the iniquity of the fathers upon the children."

It doesn't matter if your father, the idol worshipper, gave his life to Christ and became born again two days or two years before his death; the curse will keep rolling down the line unless it is prayerfully broken. God is just; He keeps His Word and stands by the law.

The gravity of the problem of inherited family curses for anyone with faulty foundations and for people of every culture of this world (not just of African origin) cannot be overemphasized. Idol worship is widespread and continues unabated until today. It is a practice common not only to poor, illiterate, and backward people but also to the most educated, sophisticated, and exposed city dwellers, who are neck-deep in idol worship, and this also includes churchgoers—both Orthodox and Pentecostal churches.

One can hardly find a home or family in Africa that did not worship idols within the last two generations. Most families had ancestral idols at their home base back in their villages (or rural areas of origin). These idols have people who minister to them and serve them on behalf of the "absentee city dwellers." Living abroad or far away from your family does not exclude you from the consequences of what has been done on your behalf; the implications are obvious. So we all have to examine our family backgrounds and check our histories for evidence or traces of idol worship and take appropriate actions to free ourselves.

Interestingly, apart from Jesus, Who was a "super deliverance Minister," there were two other powerful deliverance ministers in the Bible: Moses in the Old Testament and Paul in the New Testament. Perhaps if they had not been deliverance ministers, they would not have been successful in their missions.

Paul was a missionary to the Gentiles, who were principally idol worshippers. He had to be a deliverance minister; otherwise, he would not have been able to achieve much in his ministry. Moses, for his part, was born in Egypt, here in Africa where idol worship was the norm.

These two great men of God had revealing and insightful things to say in the Bible about demons, witchcraft, and other such phenomena. For instance, the practice of cutting marks or making incisions on the face and/or other parts of the body was (and, to an extent, still is) rampant in Africa and now has become a fashionable art form in America and all over the world (popularly known as **tattoos**). However, there is a clear warning in the law of God concerning this.

> Ye shall not make any cuttings in your flesh
> for the dead, nor print any marks upon you: I am
> the LORD. (Leviticus 19:28)

Idol worshippers are not children of God; they are clearly in league with the very forces that Paul says we war against. God hates idol worship with a sincere hatred. And the measure of His contempt for this act is evident in the book of Jeremiah, where He exposes the powerlessness of idols and the folly of their worshippers.

> For the customs of the people are vain: for
> one cutteth a tree out of the forest, the work of
> the hands of the workman, with the axe.

> They deck it with silver and with gold; they
> fasten it with nails and with hammers, that it
> move not.
> They are upright as the palm tree, but speak
> not: they must needs be borne, because they can-
> not go. Be not afraid of them; for they cannot
> do evil, neither also is it in them to do good.
> (Jeremiah 10:3–5)

This apt description mirrors a peculiar form of idolatry I have seen practiced among some tribes in Africa (specifically the Yoruba tribe of Western Nigeria), namely the worship of twins! Whenever twins are born in this particular tribe, the children are automatically named **Taiwo** (meaning **"the first of the two to have a taste of the world"**) and **Kehinde** (meaning **"the one bringing up the rear"**). In the event that one of them dies, the family makes a wooden carving called **Orisa Ibej (twin idol)** to represent the dead twin. This lifeless piece of wood then becomes an object of worship, and the family would relate to it as though it were the living sibling to the surviving twin.

Sometime ago, I was blessed with a set of twins. Just like my father who got married when he was close to fifty years of age, I also got married somewhat late in life. Since we were late starters in marriage, my wife and I prayed to God to take us through an express route so that we could have all the children we wanted before age and other natural obstacles set in. To the glory of God, He answered our prayers and gave us two boys (my twin sons).

The events that were to follow cast further light on the dangerous practice of the idol worship of twins among the Yoruba tribe of Western Nigeria. Immediately after the birth of my twins was announced, traditional dancers descended on my home, singing the praises of these little tots and calling them Orisa Meji (meaning "two idols"). But I put my foot down and said, "Not in my house!" I chased them away and cancelled their declarations in the name of Jesus.

Demonic Names

Some family curses also come from the demonic names that these families adopt, names derived from family idols. This is also common in many cultures. In America, for example, we do not attach any importance to names and their meanings; as a result, we answer to any name, good or evil. In Africa, those who worship certain rivers adopt the names of such rivers; for example, in the Yoruba tribe of Western Nigeria, we have Oshun, Osa, Okun, and so on. They use such names as prefixes to their family and first names. Other names begin with some other idols such as Sango, Ogun, Oya, Egun, Orisa, Awo, and so on.

Others believe in their family's familiar spirits (i.e., spirits that operate within the family). As a result, any child born into such a family and is perceived to resemble a dead relative (maybe grandmother or grandfather) has a special name (or prefix) attached to his or her name. This is so because the child is seen as a reincarnated being (of that dead relative); he or she becomes venerated—an object of worship. When looking at a typical Yoruba family (from the western region of Nigeria), you will most likely find someone with the name Babatunde (meaning "Father is back"), Babajide (meaning "Father has risen"), Iyabo or Yetunde (meaning "Mother has come"), Yewande ("Mother has sought me out"), and so on.

Curses Pronounced on the Family

Back in the day, there were lots of disagreements, arguments, and quarrels between families; these disagreements stemmed from bitter land disputes; wife snatching, broken marriages, and other diverse marital issues; disputes over chieftaincy titles; and all kinds of acrimonious rivalries. In the course of these quarrels, many unwholesome steps were taken by different families. Among other things, they pronounced curses on each other. Unfortunately, some of those curses have affected many lives and have continued to operate within those families. Long after the original parties in the dispute had died and the dispute has been forgotten, children born into such families continue to suffer the consequences of the curses pronounced on their ancestors.

When my father snatched my mother from her rightful husband, the man's family was not happy about it. Curses were exchanged between his family and my father's family. Although at this time I had not been born, I suffered the consequences of those curses that my father brought upon the family. Every one of his children did.

Perhaps one of the most vivid examples of how an inherited family curse can wreak havoc in the life of an innocent person is seen in one of Abraham's experiences. His story also offers us another confirmation that the Word of God will stand no matter who you are.

Abraham was a friend of God, yet he was barren well into his old age. He was not a sinner, as he conversed with God on a regular basis. However, Abraham was ignorant of the source of his problems; he had inherited a curse but was not aware of it—just like you and me. In the Bible, we see a clear pattern that confirms that Abraham's problem was inherited. His father, Terah, was an idol worshipper. The generations before his father had a record of giving birth to their first child quite early in life—between the ages of twenty-nine and thirty-five. It was Terah who broke that cycle.

> v. 12—And Arphaxad lived <u>five and thirty years</u> and begat Salah…
>
> v. 14—And Salah lived <u>thirty years</u> and begat Eber…
>
> v. 16—And Eber lived <u>four and thirty years</u> and begat Peleg…
>
> v. 18—And Peleg lived <u>thirty years</u> and begat Reu…
>
> v. 20—And Reu lived <u>two and thirty years</u> and begat Serug…
>
> v. 22—And Serug lived <u>thirty years</u> and begat Nahor…
>
> v. 24—And Nahor lived <u>nine and twenty years</u> and begat Terah…

> v. 26—And Terah lived <u>seventy years</u> and begat Abram, Nahor, and Haran. (Genesis 11:12–26)

Terah, an idol worshipper, was seventy years old when he had Abraham, meaning that he was barren for at least thirty-five years.

> And Joshua said unto all the people, Thus saith the Lord God of Israel, Your fathers dwelt on the other side of the flood in the old time, even Terah, the father of Abraham and the father of Nahor: and they served other gods. (Joshua 24:2)

The curse, therefore, started from Terah and lasted for four generations; Isaac inherited this curse, and so did Jacob, his son. Abraham, who was not a party to his father's offense, suffered for whatever it was Terah had done. And even though Abraham was so close to God that any request He made to God was answered, this physical need of his (a child) was a problem that went unanswered. Of course, God was merciful to him and subsequently answered his prayer for a child.

Note also that the length of the period of barrenness reduced with every generation.

a. Terah was barren for 35 years.
b. Abraham was barren for 25 years.
c. Isaac was barren for 20 years.
d. Jacob was barren for 7 years.

For more clarification, read the following passages:

a.	**Terah**	**Genesis 11:26**
b.	**Abraham**	**Genesis 21:5 (called at age 75)**
c.	**Abraham and Sarah**	**Genesis 12:4–5**
d.	**Isaac**	**Genesis 25:20, 21, 26**
e.	**Jacob**	**Genesis 30:1**

The curse of barrenness was not the only curse that was upon Abraham's family; there was also the curse of lying and other marital problems that came directly from Abraham's blood. With little or no prompting, Abraham lied about Sarah, his wife.

> And Abraham said of Sarah his wife, She is my sister: and Abimelech king of Gerar sent, and took Sarah. (Genesis 20:2)

Isaac inherited this lying spirit.

> And the men of the placed asked him of his wife; and he said, She is my sister: for he feared to say, She is my wife; lest, said he, the men of the place should kill me for Rebekah; because she was fair to look upon. (Genesis 26:7)

Lying was also second nature to Jacob, who lied to his old, blind father.

> And he came unto his father and said, "My father," and he said, "Here am I; who art thou, my son?"
> And Jacob said unto his father, "I am Esau thy first born; I have done according as thou badest me: arise, I pray thee, sit and eat of my venison, that thy soul may bless me." (Genesis 27:18–19)

And of course, Jacob's children lied to him cruelly when they sold their brother Joseph into slavery, making him believe that Joseph was dead. This completed the cycle of four generations of liars in Abraham's family.

Traditional Marriage Rites

For some people, diverse curses entered into their lives on the day of their traditional or cultural wedding ceremonies. In certain parts of Africa, these ceremonies usually involve the presentation of such items as kolanuts, honey, bitter kolanuts, salt, etc. In most cases, the presentation of these items has deep demonic covenants attached to them.

Although the guests consume some of these items after the ceremony, family representatives would send portions of the items to their hometowns or villages to be offered to some family idol or *juju*. In most cases, the newlyweds are not aware of this. The bride and groom then proceed to the church to carry out the Christian wedding ceremony, unaware of the covenant that has been made on their marriage.

Naturally, as Christians, the couples move on with their lives, expecting to be blessed by the same God Who violently detests any contact with the idols that they have unknowingly made a pact with! Straight from church, some couples are paraded before people chanting their "praise names" (*oriki*). Among the Yoruba tribe of Western Nigeria, this is a lengthy poem or singing the praises of a person and his ancestral lineage, going back several generations. Unfortunately, none of these *oriki* give praises to God or to Jesus, just to idols and demons.

As the man's ego becomes boosted by this relentless infusion of flattery and praise singing, what is actually happening is that the demons ruling the family have already possessed him and have begun to manifest themselves in his body. As you receive the praise, you also activate the curses that run in your family, which have now been empowered to operate in your life. This is one of the methods by which people transfer and renew curses in their families.

CHAPTER 8

Victory in the Blood of Jesus

Ordinarily, blood is a mysterious substance. The very sight of blood brings to mind all kinds of serious connotations, especially as it is intricately tied to life and death. In the history of creation, it is recorded that God formed man from the dust; he had no life in him until God breathed upon him and he became a living soul. Immediately, the spirit came upon man, and blood started to carry his life.

> For the life of the flesh is in the blood...
> (Leviticus 17:11)

If the blood carries life, we can then conclude that life's very essence is in the blood. The Bible records that when God established His covenant with Noah, telling him what he could and could not eat, He specifically warned him against eating meat that still had blood in it because "the life is in the blood."

> But flesh with the life thereof, which is the
> blood thereof, shall ye not eat. (Genesis 9:4)

Blood is life!

> Then I passed by and saw you kicking about
> in your blood, and as you lay there in your blood
> I said to you, "Live!" (Ezekiel 16:6 NIV)

> For the life of the flesh is in the blood: and
> I have given it to you upon the altar to make
> atonement for your souls: for it is the blood that
> maketh atonement for the soul. (Leviticus 17:11)

So it is a divine decision that the blood will atone for the soul. The Bible also says,

> And almost all things are by the law purged
> with blood; and without the shedding of blood is
> no remission. (Hebrews 9:22)

When Adam fell, God Himself had to slaughter an animal and use the skin to clothe Adam and his wife, Eve, thus passing through the bloodline again.

> Because the life of every creature is its blood.
> That is why I have said to the Israelites, "You
> must not eat the blood of any creature, because
> the life of every creature is its blood; anyone who
> eats it must be cut off." (Leviticus 17:14 NIV)

The Bible says that life is in the blood. When God created man in the beginning, it just lay there lifeless until the Lord breathed into his nostrils. The breath of God made man a living soul; therefore, the life and soul of man are in the blood. Blood is one of the mysterious things created by the Almighty God.

> And there are three that bear witness in
> earth, the Spirit, and the water, and the blood:
> and these three agree in one. (1 John 5:8)

Here we see the importance of the blood. God spoke many other things into being during creation, but He created man with His own hands—that's why the Bible says "we are fearfully and wonderfully made." God breathed His life into man, and that life is held in the blood, thus making man more wonderful than angels who have no flesh or blood.

In medical science, we are told that the blood is a living liquid; it is alive. It is the blood that carries oxygen from the lungs to all parts of the body, so while you are inhaling and exhaling, the air you breathe goes into your blood, which circulates it throughout the body. It is the blood that conveys the food you eat to various parts of the body. It is also the blood that helps excrete waste materials from the body. Blood is an agent of purification; it helps maintain the water content of the body.

In the blood, there are cells that constantly attack sicknesses and weaknesses in the blood. The same blood can serve as an emergency first-aid material. It is the power plant of the body. Medical practitioners say that each cell in the body receives new blood every 250 seconds, so that makes the blood a very powerful equipment and instrument. In spite of the great advancement in medicine, the blood is still not fully understood, so if you meet a person losing blood, he is dying gradually.

Mysteries about the blood

1. Shedding of blood is forbidden.
2. Shedding of innocent blood is forbidden. When Jesus appeared before Pilate, he said,

> And the governor said, "Why, what evil
> hath he done?" But they cried out the more,
> saying, "Let him be crucified." When Pilate saw

that he could prevail nothing, but that rather a tumult was made, he took water and washed his hands before the multitude, saying, "I am innocent of the blood of this just person: see yet to it." Then answered all the people and said, "His blood be on us, and on our children." (Matthew 27:23–25)

The Jews were aware of the law that forbids the shedding of innocent blood.

3.   The blood speaks, and because of the life in it, it can communicate.

And He said, "What hast thou done? The voice of thy brother's blood crieth unto me from the ground." (Genesis 4:10)

The blood of Abel was crying out for vengeance.

Covenants

There is a positive (or good) covenant and a negative covenant. God promised to deliver the prisoners who have been put in the pit where there is no water. The positive covenant is what Jesus achieved for us by His death on the cross. The first question to ask is, what is a covenant?

A covenant is a mutual agreement between two parties; it signifies a mutual understanding between two or more parties. It can be designed to achieve friendship or procure assistance in war. It can be done for mutual protection or to establish peace. A covenant can be done in several other ways, but it is a legal contract, a binding agreement, or solemn agreement.

In the Old Testament, when a Hebrew talks about a covenant, he is actually talking about cutting an animal in two and making both parties involved in the covenant pass between it. This is why they use the phrase "cutting a covenant." The general purpose of a covenant, therefore, is to provide a binding sense of commitment. God is the Originator of covenants; whenever He wants to finally commit Himself to a thing, He enters into a covenant.

A covenant is a strong thing binding two parties like a contract or a treaty. The terms of the covenant are usually spelt out; breaking them is a very serious matter. Although some physical activities are involved, a covenant is a spiritual thing.

> Now when I passed by thee, and looked upon thee, behold, thy time was the time of love; and I spread my skirt over thee, and covered thy nakedness: yea, I sware unto thee, and entered into a covenant with thee, saith the Lord God, and thou becamest mine. (Ezekiel 16:8)

> Behold, the days come, saith the Lord, that I will sow the house of Israel and the house of Judah with the seed of man, and with the seed of beast. And it shall come to pass, that like as I have watched over them, to pluck up, and to break down, and to throw down, and to destroy, and to afflict; so will I watch over them, to build, and to plant, saith the Lord. In those days they shall say no more, "The fathers have eaten sour grape, and the children's teeth are set on edge." But everyone shall doe for his own iniquity: every man that eateth the sour grape, his teeth shall be set on edge. Behold, the days come, saith the Lord, that I will make a new covenant with the house of Israel, and with the house of Judah: Not according to the covenant that I made with their fathers in the day that I took them by the hand to bring them out of the land of Egypt; which My covenant they brake, although I was an husband unto them, saith the Lord: But this shall be the covenant that

I will make with the house of Israel; After those days, saith the Lord, I will put my law in their inward parts, and write it in their hearts; and will be their God, and they shall be My people. And they shall teach no more ever man his neighbour, and every man his brother, saying, "Know the Lord": for they shall all know Me, from the least of them unto the greatest of them, saith the Lord: for I will forgive their iniquity, and I will remember their sin no more. (Jeremiah 31:27–34)

And ye shall circumcise the flesh of your foreskin; and it shall be a token of the covenant betwixt me and you. (Genesis 17:11)

Throughout the Bible, you will find many covenants between God and man—for example, the covenant of circumcision between God and Abraham. Circumcision involves shedding of blood, and to date, the Jews still keep this covenant, which is one of the reasons why Israel is a special nation. As long as they do not break the Abrahamic covenant, they cannot be defeated by another nation. It is therefore unprofitable for any nation to stand against Israel because God declared,

And I will bless them that bless thee, and curse him that curseth thee... (Genesis 12:3)

The power of covenants

When two people make a covenant, they become legal representatives of their families (or people connected to them), even unborn children and the upcoming generation. In other words, a covenant entered into five hundred years ago will still be effective and working today even among children yet to be born—the covenant will be waiting for them as soon as they are born into this world. This is the power of covenants and why one has to be careful before entering into one.

CHAPTER 9

Scriptural Declaration of Victory through the Blood of Jesus

1. Through the blood of Jesus, I am redeemed out of the hand of the devil **(Ephesians 1:7)**.
2. Through the blood of Jesus, all my sins are forgiven **(Psalm 107:2)**.
3. The blood of Jesus, God's Son, continually cleanses me from all sin **(1 John 1:7)**.
4. Through the blood of Jesus, I am justified, made righteous, *just as if I'd* never sinned **(Romans 5:9)**.
5. Through the blood of Jesus, I am sanctified, made holy, and set apart unto God **(Hebrews 13:12)**.
6. My body is the temple of the Holy Spirit, redeemed and cleansed by the blood of Jesus **(1 Corinthians 6:19–20)**.
7. Satan has no place in or power over me through the blood of Jesus and the Word of God **(Revelation 12:11)**.
8. In Him (Jesus) we have redemption (deliverance and salvation) through His blood, the remission (forgiveness) of our offenses (shortcomings and trespasses), in accordance with the riches and the generosity of His gracious favor, which He lavished upon us with every kind of wisdom and understanding (practical insight and prudence) **(Ephesians 1:7–8)**.

9. Let the redeemed of the Lord say so, whom He has delivered from the hand of the adversary **(Psalm 107:2)**.

10. But if we are (really) walking and living in the Light as He (Himself) is the Light, we have (true) unbroken fellowship with one another, and the blood of Jesus Christ, His Son, cleanses (removes) us from all guilt and sin (keeps us clean from sin in all of its forms and manifestations) **(1 John 1:7)**.

11. Therefore, since we are now justified (acquitted, made righteous, and brought into a right relationship with God) by Christ's blood, how much more (certain) shall we be saved by Him from the indignation and wrath of God **(Romans 5:9)**.

12. Therefore, Jesus also suffered and died outside the (city's) gate in order that He might purify and consecrate (sanctify) the people through (the shedding of) His own blood and set them apart as holy (unto God) **(Hebrews 13:12)**.

13. Do you not know that your body is the temple (the very sanctuary) of the Holy Spirit Who lives with you and Whom you have received (as a Gift) from God? You are not your own **(1 Corinthians 6:19)**.

14. You were bought with a price (purchased with preciousness and paid for, made His own). So then, honor (your) God and bring glory to Him in your body **(1 Corinthians 6:20)**.

15. And they have overcome (conquered) him by means of the blood of the Lamb and by the utterance of their testimony, for they did not love or cling to life even when faced with death (holding their lives cheap till they had to die for their witnessing) **(Revelation 12:11)**.

16. In the name of Jesus, O Lord, baptize me with the fire of deliverance, in the name of Jesus!

17. All demonic spirits attached to all covenants and curses, I bind you and command you to come out of my life in the name of Jesus!

18. Father, let the blood of Jesus Christ erase all my sins that opened the doors to the curses recorded in the Bible in the name of Jesus!

19. By the power of resurrection, I reverse every negative decree already signed against me and that can affect me in any form in the name of Jesus!

20. Father, reverse every negative order placed over my destiny in the name of Jesus!

21. Holy Spirit, let Your voice respond on my behalf wherever my name is written or mentioned in the name of Jesus!

22. Holy Spirit, confuse my enemies in their own camp in the name of Jesus!

23. Let the power of God tear down everything the devil has put together concerning my name in the name of Jesus!

24. Under the new covenant that is the covenant of the blood of Jesus, I renounce all the evil works I have done in the lives of innocent people through my membership with these demonic associations, and I ask the Almighty God to forgive me and cleanse me with the blood of Jesus in the name of Jesus!

25. I request the blood of Jesus to flush out my system, purify my body, and cleanse me from all evil things I have eaten in any of the demonic cults or associations in the name of Jesus!

26. Wherever my name has been initiated either consciously or unconsciously, I withdraw and cancel my name from their registers with the blood of Jesus in the name of Jesus!

27. By the power in the blood of Jesus, I withdraw any part of my body or blood deposited on their evil altars in the name of Jesus!

28. I withdraw pictures, objects, presentations, food, sacrifices, money, children, wife, husband, clothes, images, and any other personal belongings from the altars of the forces of darkness in the name of Jesus!

29. I return any weapon (physical or spiritual) belonging to the kingdom of darkness that I was a part of, and I also return

any other properties for the execution of satanic duties at my disposal in the name of Jesus!

30. Holy Spirit, build a wall of fire around me and let there be a permanent disconnection between the satanic kingdom and me in the name of Jesus!

31. By the blood of Jesus, I cancel and erase every evil mark, incision, tattoo, and writing inserted on my body as a result of my participation with the forces of darkness in the name of Jesus!

32. I break all covenants that I have undertaken for my children, grandchildren, and generations after me in the name of Jesus!

33. By the power in the blood of Jesus, I renounce and denounce every dedication of my destiny to any river, mountain, or idol in the place of my birth in the name of Jesus!

34. By the power in the blood of Jesus, I renounce and denounce every initiation into occultism by my parents and/or grandparents in the name of Jesus!

35. By the power in the blood of Jesus, I cancel every dedication or covenant with family idols, evil trees, forests, markets, road junctions, and so on in the name of Jesus!

36. Anyone monitoring me through a satanic glass or device, I command that glass or device to be broken in the name of Jesus!

CHAPTER 10

Prayers to Reverse All Curses

Having read this book up to this point, the following are prayer points that I encourage you to take up personally, and the Lord will grant you deliverance and victory in Jesus's name.

Repentance and Confession

Dear God in the name of JESUS,

1. According to **Romans 10:9**, I confess with my lips that JESUS is Lord, and in my heart, I believe that You raised Him from the dead.
2. According to **Luke 13:3**, I repent of my past sins and I admit and confess that I have sinned (mention the sin), and I believe that You are faithful and just to cleanse me from all unrighteousness.
3. I call upon You, Lord JESUS, to cleanse me from all sin and unrighteousness by Your blood **(1 John 1:7)**. And as Your Word says in **Romans 10:13**, "Everyone who calls upon the name of the Lord shall be saved."
4. I confess, repent, and ask for forgiveness from occult practices such as witchcraft, fortune telling, horoscopes, astrology, Halloween, etc.

5. I renounce Satan and all occult practices and break all curses associated with those practices. According to **Galatians 3:13**, Christ purchased our freedom (redeeming us) from the curse (doom) of the law (and its condemnation) by becoming a curse for us. For it is written (in the scriptures), "Cursed is everyone who hangs on a tree (crucified)" **(Deuteronomy 21:23)**.

6. I confess, repent, and ask for forgiveness of all sins listed in **Deuteronomy 27 and 28**, and I break the curses associated with those sins.

7. I confess, repent, and ask for forgiveness of my iniquities and my father's iniquities according to **Leviticus 26:40**, and I break the curses associated with those iniquities.

8. I break and loose myself from all evil soul ties with my mother, father, brother, sister, spouse, former spouse, former sex partners, etc.

9. Lord JESUS, I forgive my mother, father, brothers (mention their names), sisters (mention their names), and anyone else who has ever hurt my name **(Matthew 6:15, 18:21, 22, 35; Luke 11:4)** (our Lord's Prayer).

10. I break and loose myself and my family from all curses that have been or are being placed upon us—curses of witchcraft, psychic thoughts or prayers, ungodly intercessory prayers, and words spoken in anger—and I return these curses back to the sender(s) sevenfold and I bind them with the blood of Jesus.

Renouncing General and Hidden Curses

1. I break and cancel every curse placed upon me by my parents either due to their carelessness, in anger, or by mistake in the name of Jesus!

2. By the resurrection power, I deactivate the power of all curses affecting my ancestral family as a result of their sin and disobedience to God in the name of Jesus!

3. I break and cancel every curse, evil pronouncement, spells, hexes, enchantment, bewitchment, and incantations placed upon me by the kingdom of darkness in the name of Jesus!

4. I break and revoke every blood and soul-tie covenants and yokes attached to those curses in the name of Jesus!

5. I purge myself of all evil foods I have eaten with the blood of Jesus, and I purify myself with the fire of the Holy Ghost in the name of Jesus!

6. Father, please forgive me and may the blood of Jesus cleanse me from every disobedience that introduced curses into my life in the name of Jesus!

7. Holy Ghost, revoke every caterpillar and cankerworms that are destroying my finances as a result of the curses in the book of Malachi in the name of Jesus!

8. Lord, let the blood of Jesus speak for me regarding any of the curses recorded in the Bible that is affecting my progress in the name of Jesus!

9. Holy Spirit, deliver me from all self-inflicted curses that were pronounced either consciously or unconsciously in the name of Jesus!

10. I retrieve and cancel every word I have spoken at any time of my life that has brought judgment upon me in the name of Jesus!

11. All power implementing evil curses over my life, you are defeated in the name of Jesus!

12. I return to sender every curse pronounced over my life by demonic agents of darkness in the name of Jesus!

13. I plead the blood of Jesus over all evil pronouncements affecting my destiny in the name of Jesus!

14. By the power in the blood of Jesus, I break all self-imposed curses working against my progress in the name of Jesus!

15. God of Elijah, arise and deliver me from every curse of polygamy in my foundation in the name of Jesus!

16. By the blood of Jesus, I break every curse used by the strongmen of my father's house in the name of Jesus!

17. By the blood of Jesus, I break every curse used by the strongmen of my mother's house in the name of Jesus!
18. By the power in the blood of Jesus, I break every curse of untimely death working in my family line in the name of Jesus!
19. By the power in the blood of Jesus, I break every curse of wrong marriages in my family line—I decree that I am not your candidate in the name of Jesus!
20. By the power in the blood of Jesus, I terminate every curse of stubborn limitations in my family line in the name of Jesus!
21. Under the covenant of the blood of Jesus, I stand to neutralize and deactivate the power of every curse inflicted on me at any point in time because Christ has redeemed me from the curse of the law.

Deliverance from Generational Curses

1. Holy Ghost, scatter all powers inherited from my parents, propelling my life toward a direction not commissioned by God, in the name of Jesus!
2. I destroy all evil powers implementing evil decrees into my life in the name of Jesus!
3. I command all powers of darkness assigned to implement failure in my life to come out of my life in the name of Jesus!
4. I scatter every gathering of the ungodly against me, physically or spiritually, from my conception till this present day in the name of Jesus!
5. Every form of evil information brought against me from the kingdom of darkness, I cancel you in the name of Jesus!
6. I abort every operation of the forces of darkness commissioned against me to monitor my progress in life in the name of Jesus!
7. (Lay your right hand on your head and your other hand on your stomach.) Every evil operation, evil nature, and

evil habits inherited from my lineage, lose your hold in the name of Jesus!

8. Every initiation, dedication, and manipulation that has yoked me into all forms of generational bondage, be broken now and forever in the name of Jesus!

9. Let every incantation, evil decrees, and curses uttered against me from my birth become impotent in the name of Jesus!

10. All curses affecting the members of my family, lose your grip and hold over my life in the name of Jesus!

11. I paralyze the activities of every strongman ruling over my generation and working against my progress in the name of Jesus!

12. Let every generational curse that is affecting my destiny be broken in the name of Jesus!

13. I renounce all curses originating from my ancestors—I denounce the power of those curses in the name of Jesus!

14. I break all evil pronouncements propelling my life to the same type of failure, misfortune, poverty, and material lack suffered by my ancestors in the name of Jesus!

15. Holy Ghost, disconnect me from all curses placed upon my ancestral family that is now affecting my progress in the name of Jesus!

16. By the power in the blood of Jesus, I paralyze all foundational curses working against my divine destiny in the name of Jesus!

17. By the power in the blood of Jesus, I break all generational curses of poverty, mutilating against my breakthroughs, in the name of Jesus!

18. By the power in the blood of the Lamb, I paralyze every parental curse hindering my progress in the name of Jesus!

19. By the power in the blood of the Lamb, I break the generational curse of idolatry working against my life in the name of Jesus!

20. I release myself and my family from all collective captivity of idolatry in the place of my birth in the wonderful name of Jesus!

21. By the power in the blood of Jesus, I release myself and my family from the collective captivity of innocent blood that was shed by my parents up to ten generations ago in the name of Jesus!

22. I break the power of every foundational curse placed on the place of my birth in the name of Jesus!

23. By the power in the blood of Jesus, I paralyze every curse of "aborted destinies" in my family line, and I declare that I am not your CANDIDATE in the name of Jesus!

Breaking Evil Covenants and Curses

1. I break the curses of idle words and abominations that caused generations before me to go after the gods of this world in the name of Jesus!

2. I break the curse of idolatry and paganistic practices and command them to lose their hold on my life in the name of Jesus!

3. I break the curses of "the wanderer and the vagabond." I break every curse of rebellion, disobedience, and not obeying the Word of God. I command selfishness and greed to lose their hold on me in the name of Jesus!

4. I break the curse of the city where I was born and everything that has affected me from that city in the name of Jesus!

5. I break every curse on my fields, lands, and inheritance. I break every curse on the fruit of my body, on my children, and on my generation in the name of Jesus!

6. I break every curse concerning the work of my hands, the increase of my wealth, and the blessings of my land in the name of Jesus!

7. I break all curses on my going out and my coming in, on my sitting down and my rising up in the name of Jesus!

8. I break the curse on my basket and my storehouse in the name of Jesus!

9. I break every curse set up by Satan to bring defeat into my generation in the name of Jesus!

10. I command all lawlessness and rebellion to cease in the name of Jesus!

11. I break the curse of confusion. I command the spirit of confusion, the spirit of Babylon—the harlot system, the whorish nature of the flirtatious woman that goes whoring after other gods—to lose its hold on my life right now in the name of Jesus!

12. I come against the curse of Babylon. I go back four generations and break its hold on my life in the name of Jesus!

13. I come against all rebuke, blasphemy, and every curse of damnation that has been spoken against my bloodline for the past four generations in the name of Jesus!

14. I break everything that took away my self-worth in the name of Jesus!

15. I come against the spirit of destruction. I command this curse of destruction to be loosed from my generation in the mighty name of Jesus!

16. I command the curse of all forms of evil—backbiting, slander, contention, anger, hatred, and so on—to come out in the name of Jesus!

17. I come against every pestilence. I break the curse of poverty and command it to lose its hold on my life in the name of Jesus!

18. I break the curses of stealing and deceit, incest, illegitimacy, and sodomy. I come against the spirits of pride and self-righteousness. I command all religious spirits to lose their hold on my life. Everything that has been stolen from me, I command an immediate restoration in the name of Jesus!

19. I break the curses of consumption and fever, inflammation, fiery heat, sword and drought, blasting and mildew,

which continue to pursue me. I come against all diseases and infirmities in the name of Jesus!

20. I break the curse of brass—not hearing, no sight, no vision—in the name of Jesus!

21. I command condemnation to lose its hold on my life in the name of Jesus!

22. I break the curse of powdered soil and dust from the heavens in the name of Jesus!

23. I break the curse that causes me to be struck down by my enemies. I command the spirits of failure and lack of vision to lose its hold on my life in the name of Jesus!

24. I break the curse of premature death and the curse of boils, blood diseases, and tumors in the name of Jesus!

25. I lose the curse of cancer from my body in the name of Jesus!

26. I command bitterness (the roots of bitterness), resentment, and unforgiveness to lose its hold on my life. I break the curse of molestation and frigidity in the name of Jesus!

27. I break everything that would make me the tail (i.e., beneath always) in the name of Jesus!

28. I come against depression, insanity, and retardation in the name of Jesus!

29. Under the covering of the blood of Jesus, I break the curse of scurvy, itching, all skin diseases, herpes, psoriasis, and all infirmities or conditions that don't heal. I come against the torment of itching and nervousness in the name of Jesus!

30. I break the curse of shingles, madness, and insanity in the name of Jesus!

31. I break the curse of blindness and no spiritual insight in the name of Jesus!

32. I come against the spirit of dismay, despair, mental anguish, and mental depression in the name of Jesus!

33. By the power in the blood of Jesus, I cancel everything that has bruised my life as a result of generational curses in the name of Jesus!

34. I call on heaven and earth to witness that I will no longer be bound by poverty. I come against the enemy coming in and robbing me of all things that are precious and good in the name of Jesus!

35. I break the curse of lust, promiscuity, adultery, fornication, bestiality, and perversion. I cancel your assignments in my life in the name of Jesus!

36. I break the curse of sore boils in the knees and legs, causing a lack of balance. I decree healing from the crown of my head to the soles of my feet in the name of Jesus!

37. I break the curse of all the diseases of Egypt and all types of diseases which could run in my bloodline—arthritis, diabetes, hypertension, heart trouble, nervousness, and all other blood-related diseases, weakness in the knees, rheumatism, neck and back aches, and pain in the spinal cord—in the name of Jesus!

38. I break the curse of edema and swelling. I command heart attack and stroke to be broken off from my bloodline in the name of Jesus!

39. I break the curse that would allow the enemy to pursue and overtake me in the name of Jesus!

40. I break all curses of mind control and witchcraft in my bloodline, and I command every demon to lose its hold over my life in the name of Jesus!

41. I break every curse pronounced into my life by false prophets, and I command that all false teachings and errors that I have heard and accepted be cancelled and removed from my life in the name of Jesus!

42. I break the curse of unbelievers in my household—from the lives of my father, mother, siblings, children, husband or wife—in the name of Jesus!

43. I break the curse of laziness and I command the spirit of passivity to lose its hold on my life in the name of Jesus!

44. I command the witch, the warlock, and the generation that has been filtered with these evils to depart in the name of Jesus!

45. I break the curse of the spirit of Jezebel, and I lose that theatrical spirit that always wants to be seen and heard in the name of Jesus!

46. I break the curse of verbal and physical abuse (many times as children, we were whipped or beaten and verbally abused, and this has left a mark on our personality). I come against the spirit of abuse and break the curses of damnation in the name of Jesus!

47. O Lord, baptize me with the fire of deliverance in the name of Jesus!

48. I bind all demonic spirits attached to covenants and curses and command you to come out of my life in the name of Jesus!

49. Father, let the blood of Jesus erase all my sins that opened the doors to the curses recorded in the Bible in the name of Jesus!

50. By the power of resurrection, I reverse every negative decree already signed against me and that can affect me in any form in the name of Jesus!

51. Father, reverse every negative order placed over my destiny in the name of Jesus!

52. Holy Spirit, wherever my name has been written or is mentioned, let Your voice respond on my behalf in the name of Jesus!

53. Holy Spirit, confuse my enemies in their own camp in the name of Jesus!

54. Let the power of God tear down everything the devil has put together concerning my name in the name of Jesus!

55. Under the new covenant, which is the covenant of the blood of Jesus, I renounce all the evil works I have done in the lives of innocent people through my membership with these demonic associations, and I ask the Almighty God to forgive me and cleanse me with the blood of Jesus in the name of Jesus!

56. I request the blood of Jesus to flush out my system, purify my body, and cleanse me from all evil things I have eaten

in any of the demonic cults or associations in the name of
Jesus!

57. Wherever my name has been initiated either consciously or
unconsciously, I withdraw and cancel my name from their
registers with the blood of Jesus in the name of Jesus!

Binding and Loosing

1. I lose myself from the bonds of Satan around my neck in
the name of Jesus!

2. By the power of the Holy Ghost, I tie down the enemies in
the spirit realm in the name of Jesus!

3. I reverse the words of those who cursed me, sent evil against
me, and sent evil against the work of the Lord. I send all
their evil back to them seven times in the name of Jesus!
May the Lord Jesus bring them to their knees to repentance
so that they might be saved, healed, filled, and delivered in
the name of Jesus!

4. I reverse every assignment, trap, snare, wiles, and evil plan
or attack against me by Satan and his angels, demons,
imps, principalities, powers, rulers of the darkness of this
world, spiritual hosts of wickedness in heavenly places or
evil spirits of any kind. I silence their words and/or curses
in the name of Jesus!

5. I clothe all satanic networks with confusion as with a man-
tle. I cancel all assignments against me. By the power of
the blood of Jesus, I render all curses null and void in the
name of Jesus!

6. I ask the Lord to send legions of angels to minister to me,
protect me, fight for me, minister healing and restoration,
and surround me in the name of Jesus!

7. O God, help me to be strong in the Lord and in His power,
to exercise the authority over the devil which You have given
me, to stand against the devil, to daily put on the whole
armor of God, to pray without ceasing and intercede, and
to fight the good fight of faith in the name of Jesus!

8. I use our weapons of warfare against the kingdom of darkness, and I return all curses and demons back to sender in the name of Jesus!

9. Satan, I close every door you may have opened for evil contacts to come into my life in the name of Jesus! Because Jesus Christ became a curse on the cross for me, blotting out the handwriting of ordinances against me.

10. I break all curses dating back to the time of Adam and Eve in the Garden of Eden, and I destroy all legal grounds that the enemy has (and uses) to work with in my life in the name of Jesus!

11. I break all demonic soul-ties and bind all powers of the evil spirits and lose myself from their hold in the name of Jesus!

12. I ask for the necessary spiritual gifts, especially the gift of discernment, in the name of Jesus!

13. Having been given power and authority over Satan and his army, I ask for the anointing of the Holy Spirit to come upon me now in the name of Jesus!

14. I command the angels to turn the minds of the demons upside down, to chase and harass them, to bruise, crush, and flatten the heads of the serpentine spirits, and to snip off the tails of the scorpion spirits in the name of Jesus!

15. I order the princes and rulers of darkness to be bound with chains and thrown down before the other spirits with the words "Jesus Christ is my Lord" written in red letters on their foreheads in the name of Jesus!

16. I command the lesser spirits to attack the traitors in the camp and throw them out in the name of Jesus!

17. I command every demonic accusation against me to face God's judgment in the name of Jesus!

18. I send the warrior angels with swords to chain the rulers of darkness and throw the fire of God on them in the name of Jesus!

19. Satan, you have been defeated by Jesus, so you **must obey** His commands!

20. I bind all powers of darkness operating over my area of location, and I break the assignments from the powers of darkness in the heavens and command the ruling spirits to cast out their underlings in the name of Jesus!

21. I command the angel of the Lord to assist in my deliverance as directed by God in the name of Jesus!

22. I break evil curses, vexes, hexes, jinxes, psychic powers, bewitchment, potions, charms, incantations, spells, and witchcraft and sorcery in the name of Jesus!

23. I break all cords, snares, controls, and bondages from my life, and I ask that the power of God will be manifested in me. I command the demons that have been harassing my life to go to Tartarus with the other fallen angels in the name of Jesus!

24. I agree with the covenant of the blood of Jesus, and I use the Psalms as imprecations and pronouncements against the enemies of God. I call down the wrath of God upon all spiritual foes in the name of Jesus!

25. I come against unholy spirits, fallen angels, demons, devils, evil empires, and the entire kingdom of Satan within humans and animals. I come against councils, principalities, powers, world rulers, and wicked spirits in heavenly places in the name of Jesus!

26. I come against chiefs and kings, princes, kingdoms, dominions, generals, rulers, captains, centurions, and strongmen assigned over my life, and I command them to be destroyed in the name of Jesus!

27. I pray for healing from the damages in my life caused by these demons in the name of Jesus!

28. I bind all remaining demons or their operations until they are all cast out or they leave of their own accord in the name of Jesus!

29. I ask angels to be stationed on my properties to stand guard or keep watch in the name of Jesus!

30. I allow godly spirits from the Lord to operate in my life in the name of Jesus!

31. I agree to cleanse my being, possessions, and home of all unclean objects in the name of Jesus!

Lord, Fight for Me

1. O Lord, forgive us for our sins and the sins of our fathers in the name of Jesus!
2. O Lord, help us to return to You and keep Your commandments in the name of Jesus!
3. O Lord, let Your favor and mercy be upon us in the name of Jesus!
4. My God will commission me this year for His divine purpose in the name of Jesus!
5. Hear me, O my God! Let the hands of my enemies be weakened in the work that they are carrying out against me so it will not be done in the name of Jesus!
6. O Lord, expose my enemies and bring their plot against me to nothing in the name of Jesus!
7. O Lord, strengthen my hands to perform the work you have assigned to me in the name of Jesus!
8. Remember me, O God, for good in the name of Jesus!
9. The Lord will build a wall around me in the name of Jesus!
10. O Lord, deal with my enemies for me while I am doing the work You committed into my hands in the name of Jesus!
11. My enemies will be shocked and amazed to see how God will surprise me in the name of Jesus!
12. O Lord, redeem me by Your great power and by Your strong hand according to Your promise in the name of Jesus!
13. O Lord, give me favor in the sight of my helpers in the name of Jesus!
14. O God of heaven, cause me to prosper in the name of Jesus!
15. O Lord, remember Your servants and spare them in Your mercy in the name of Jesus!
16. Hear me, O my God, for I am despised and turn my enemy's reproach onto their own heads in the name of Jesus!

17. O Lord, send my enemies into the land of captivity in the name of Jesus!

18. I bless Your name, O Lord, for Your goodness upon my life, and I thank You for my answered prayers in the name of Jesus!

Prayers for a Fresh Start

1. Every evil handwriting written by the devil, demons, or anyone against me concerning my life, destiny, career, family, children, etc., I erase such handwriting in the name of Jesus.

2. Dear God, just as You made a way for the children of Israel, make a way for me where there seems to be no way in the name of Jesus.

3. Dear God, every enemy of progress fighting against my success or progress in life,—physically or spiritually in any form or realm—I command the earth to open its mouth and swallow them up in the name of Jesus.

4. Every evil word spoken against me in open or in secret, I condemn by the precious blood of Jesus in the name of Jesus.

5. Dear God, every wickedness sent or targeted against me in the physical or spiritual realm, I command such wickedness to perish by the fire of the Holy Ghost in the name of Jesus.

6. Every demonic oppression affecting my life, I break its power and hold over my life in the name of Jesus.

7. Every spirit of oppression and depression destroying my life, making life unbearable for me, I bind and cast you out of my life into the bottomless pit in the name of Jesus.

8. Every covenant made knowingly or unknowingly by me, my parents, or within my generation that is evil and does not bring glory to God, I break such covenants in the name of Jesus.

9. I shall succeed, I shall progress in the name of Jesus.

10. I seal my life, marriage, career, etc., with the blood of Jesus in the name of Jesus.

11. Dear God, preserve my soul from evil and destruction in the name of Jesus.

12. I cover myself with the blood of Jesus against any plan of evil or destruction or death in the name of Jesus (make this your daily prayer for protection).

13. Dear God, I know You have a plan for my life, Father. Let me walk in the plan You've made for me and my spouse, children, etc., in the name of Jesus.

14. Dear God, let Your plan for my life come to manifestation in the name of Jesus.

15. Dear God, increase Your love in me in the name of Jesus.

16. Dear God, make me RAW (ready, able, and willing) to show and practice Your love and Your will according to Your commandment in the name of Jesus.

17. Dear God, speak to me today—I want to know the right plan and direction I should follow in the name of Jesus.

18. Dear God, set me on fire for You in the name of Jesus.

19. Dear God, grant me Your divine favor to succeed and stand out amongst the crowd in the name of Jesus.

20. Pray on **Job 22:28** and begin to decree good things into your life—whatever you want Him to do for you in area of your life.

> Thou shalt also decree a thing, and it shall
> be established unto thee: and the light shall shine
> upon thy ways.

Possessing Your Possession

1. Let the anointing of special favor fall upon my life in the name of Jesus!

2. My star, arise and shine and fall no more in the name of Jesus!

3. O Lord, like Joseph, move me from the prison to the palace in the name of Jesus!

4. O God of Elijah, bury my failures in the name of Jesus!

5. If I have left my place of blessing, O Lord, take me back there by fire in the name of Jesus!

6. O Lord, as You parted the Red Sea, separate affliction from my destiny in the name of Jesus!

7. My heavenly Father, open my eyes to see my breakthroughs in the name of Jesus!

8. Let my season of divine intervention appear in the name of Jesus!

9. O Lord, open my eyes to behold wondrous treasures in the name of Jesus!

10. O Lord, cancel my journey of backwardness in the name of Jesus!

11. I command my glory to appear in the name of Jesus!

12. Angels of God, pursue my helpers and lead them to me in the name of Jesus!

13. Every Haaman assigned to kill me shall die in my place in the name of Jesus!

14. I command every satanic engineer and engine assigned against me to be destroyed in the name of Jesus!

15. I arrest the traffic of demons directed against me in the name of Jesus!

16. I command you, power of the night, from attacking my life, to turn around and begin to attack yourself in the name of Jesus!

17. O Lord, as You killed all the firstborn of the Egyptians, kill every power that wants to terminate my destiny in the name of Jesus!

18. I command every power defiling my body to die in the name of Jesus!

19. Fire of God, arise and locate the camp of my enemies in the name of Jesus!

20. I command any power redirecting my star to die in the name of Jesus!

21. Let anyone staying awake to do me harm receive an angelic slap in the name of Jesus!
22. Let the blood of Jesus wash off every strange touch of evil in my life in the name of Jesus!
23. Any material carved against me, begin to attack the manufacturer in the name of Jesus!
24. I command every altar that is raised up against me to crumble now in the name of Jesus!
25. Every priest of the night ministering against me, receive the spirit of confusion in the name of Jesus!
26. All my blessings that have been taken to the grave by any evil dead relative, arise and locate me in the name of Jesus!

Begin to thank God for answering your prayers. Sing a song of praise about the blood of Jesus. Confess and claim the promises in **Galatians 3:13–14** and **Revelation 12:11**.

Claim your total deliverance as you cover yourself, your family, your ministry, your job, your prosperity, and everything that concerns you with the blood of Jesus in the name of Jesus! Amen.

Realign Yourself into God's Presence

> And David recovered all that the Amalekites had carried away: and David rescued his two wives. And there was nothing lacking to them, neither small nor great, neither sons nor daughters, neither spoil, nor any thing that they had taken to them: David recovered all. (1 Samuel 30:18–19)

1. Lord, I thank You for Your presence in my life in the name of Jesus!
2. O God, I want to be concerned with Your issues in the name of Jesus!
3. Father, give me an understanding of Who You are in the name of Jesus!

4. Open my eyes to see what matters to You the most in the name of Jesus!

5. Lord, help me to recover what matters to You in the name of Jesus!

6. Lord, I take up Your yoke and I reject my yoke in the name of Jesus!

7. Help me to obey You in order to have a better life in the name of Jesus!

8. Lord, do something new in my life today in the name of Jesus!

9. O Lord, give me insights into Your purpose for my life in the name of Jesus!

10. My God, teach me how to fight the good fight of faith in the name of Jesus!

11. O God, send down help from above in the name of Jesus!

12. Holy Ghost, connect me to that man or woman whom You have positioned for my promotion in the name of Jesus!

13. Father, search my heart and visit my spirit man. Show me who I am and let me know Who You are in the name of Jesus!

14. Thank You for answering my prayers in the name of Jesus!

AUTHOR'S BIOGRAPHY

Rev. James A. Solomon is the President of Jesus People's Revival Ministries Inc., as well as the General Overseer and Senior Pastor of Jesus Family Chapel, with 38+ branches, in Nigeria, the United Kingdom and several other countries. The international headquarters for both ministries is based in Atlanta, Georgia, in the United States of America, where he currently resides.

Rev. Solomon is a man who is truly gifted with an extraordinary anointing on the subject of Spiritual Warfare, Healing and Deliverance. In his efforts to serve the body of Christ beyond his own ministries, he also serves as director for the West African Regional Directorate of the International Accelerated Missions (I.A.M.), a network of missionary churches based in New York.

Rev. Solomon started from very humble beginnings in his native country of Nigeria, West Africa, way back in the 1980s. With his team of ministers and due to popular demand, he has taken the revelation of Spiritual Warfare and Deliverance to massive venues such as the stadium domes in the major cities of Nigeria. He has also conducted a series of conferences, and organized quarterly Deliverance Night Services in the United Kingdom, Europe, Canada, Japan and all over the United States. Many have received freedom from satanic bondage and oppression at these quarterly deliverance services. He is in high demand as a guest minister in many crusades and conferences.